HOW TO RAISE NIGERIAN DWARF GOAT

A COMPLETE GUIDE FOR BEGINNERS

Copyright@2023

Gray Shirley

TABLE OF CONTENT

CHAPTER ONE

NIGERIAN MIDGET GOATS
INTRODUCTION

The earliest Nigerian Dwarf goats

were raised in West Africa, and they

were appreciated for their ease of care

in harsh environments, as well as their

ability to produce meat and milk

while requiring less food than other

goats. From the beginning through the

middle of the 20th century, goats were

delivered to American zoos on the

same ships as huge cats and African predators. Users were intended to be an easy-to-maintain food source for African prey crossing the ocean. Many goats survived the journey and settled in American zoos, where their small size and affectionate disposition made them enormously popular in petting zoos. As if miniaturized, the ratios of Nigerian Miniature goats seem to be more sensitive than those of regular goats. The Nigerian Dwarf goat is a versatile, reduced animal that thrives in a wide range of environments. Known for being sociable and pleasant, their small size makes them easier to care for than comparatively large species, requiring less space and less food. As with all goats, Nigerian Dwarfs are pack animals that will not be healthy or content if kept alone. If you are keeping a Nigerian Dwarf as a pet, he or she will likely not do well in an environment where he or she is left alone for long periods of time. Keeping them with other goats, or even grazing animals or dogs, will help satisfy this outgoing animal's social needs.

NIGERIAN MIDGET GOAT USES

On a small farm, Nigerian Dwarf goats are popular due to their general utility and pleasant disposition, rather than for any particular purpose.

- Like with all goats, Nigerian Dwarf goats are excellent in pastures for removing weeds and undergrowth and improving grazing conditions for animals. Due to their gentle disposition, they can be kept with grazing animals without special care or housing.

- They are qualified for 4H projects as some cattle breed. Children's programs such as 4H and FFA can benefit greatly from their small size and manageability.

- For their size, they produce a sufficient amount of high-quality milk. Its milk has a remarkable amount of butterfat, making it ideal for goat cheese, creams, and other goat milk products.

- They are polyestrous and capable of reproduction throughout the year, therefore a small number of does can maintain a constant milk supply.

- A small herd can increase rapidly, or kids and can be sold as pets, because they normally have 3-5 offspring every kidding.

- They are incredibly popular as pets and companion animals, and their small size makes them easier to keep in urban environments.

- They are fantastic animals for goat yoga

- For those who currently own a little or large farm, it is straightforward to add Nigerian Dwarf goats and reap their numerous benefits. A Nigerian Dwarf goat does not, however, require considerably additional territory or maintenance than other dog breeds for those seeking a playful, affectionate, and endearing companion.

As noted above, there are two unique class standards for Nigerian Dwarf goats. The American Smallholder Dairy Association and the Nigerian Midget Goat Affiliation each have separate conformation requirements.

1. Appearance

In essence, Nigerian Dwarf goats must imitate miniature counterparts of Alpine goats from Switzerland. AGA guidelines permit any coat color and make no distinction between brown and blue eyes (blue eyes are common in the breed, but uncommon in other dairy goats). The NDGA norm disallows wavy hair, a Roman nose, and hanging ears.

2. Size

Size According to AGA guidelines, Nigerian Dwarf does cannot exceed 22.5 inches in height at the withers, while bucks cannot exceed 23.5 inches. The NDGA allows does to reach a maximum height of 21 inches at the withers, whereas rams are limited to a maximum height of 23 inches.

3. Production

Nigerian Dwarf does produce 1-8 pounds of milk each day during lactation, with an average of 2.5 pounds. Late in lactation, their milk can contain up to 10% butterfat, compared to an average of 6.5%.

4. Disposition

Goats of the Nigerian Dwarf variety are renowned for being sociable, playful, and extroverted. They are receptive to voice calls and actively seek out human interaction, which they like. Many people bottle-feed them to foster human-animal attachment and make them better pets, while others believe that bottle-feeding makes them excessively dependent on humans and demanding.

Positive health effects of Nigerian Midget goat

Due to their food and behavior, most goats, especially Nigerian Dwarf, must have their hooves trimmed and dewormed periodically. The majority of individuals clip hoof every 4-8 weeks, deworm countless times annually, and vaccinate annually. Thankfully, their diminutive size makes them simple to manipulate. Ensure you have access to a veterinarian who is familiar with goats' needs.

CHAPTER TWO

A maximum of two to four kilograms of hay or natural forage should be fed daily to a goat of average size for glancing. Cattle and goats are both grazers with a four-chambered digestive. Due to its ruminant status, a goat has a very rapid digestion and consumes significantly more feed than its size would suggest.

1. Grass Used as Cow Feed

Hay and natural forage stuffs establish the mainstream of a goat's diet, in directive to prevent bloat, obesity, and other health concerns. Goats like hay composed primarily of legumes, but alfalfa and clover-containing bales are also acceptable. But, do not buy or cultivate hay that is excessively high in alfalfa or cover if the same hay will be fed to non-ruminant livestock, such as horses. Alfalfa hay contains a greater proportion of minerals, protein, and vitamins than is required for ruminant livestock to consume a healthy diet. Also, the calcium content of alfalfa hay is quite advantageous for nursing doe goats. To maintain a properly functioning rumen, goats must consume sufficient roughage. For the bacteria-rich rumen of the first stomach compartment to function, long-fiber hay is required. When the fur is carefully stroked, this big rumen chamber should have a "spongy" quality.

2. Feeding Chaffhaye

In addition to regular hay and grain, Chaffhaye is an excellent supplement for goats. This sort of hay is produced by cutting tall grass or alfalfa early and combining it with Bacillus subtilis (a probiotic culture) and molasses. In my rural location, it is difficult to find this type of hay in agricultural supply stores, therefore add a small amount of molasses to goat feed once each week. When there is a pregnant or nursing nanny, more frequently. Because chaffhaye is more nutrient-dense than standard pasture-baled hay, a 50-pound bale is equivalent to over 100 pounds of traditional hay.

3. Granular Goat Feed

A goat herd's hay and glance feeding habits should be supplemented with grain feed or all stock feed. Instead of allowing the goats to become too accustomed to the sweet flavor of the grain feed alone, it is strongly recommended to combine it with cracked corn. Cracked corn will subsidize more nutrients to the herd's diet than all-stock or sweet mix grain feed alone. During warm-weather months, grain is typically offered as a treat or as a modest dietary supplement, unless there is insufficient land for goats to graze in addition to being fed hay bales. During the colder months, grain feed rations are raised to provide animals with a greater amount of minerals, protein, vitamins, and other nutrients. During the summer, a cup of grain per day to my dwarf goat breeds. Two cups may be safely administered to a goat of average size. But, this is only a pleasure for my privileged herd, since they have free access to over 56 acres for browse, and not a necessity for their diet. Grain feed should be carefully monitored to prevent overfeeding, which can not only result in potentially disastrous bloat, but also colic.

4. Nutrients for Goats

The goats should have year-round access to mineral blocks and a salt block during the warmer months at the very least. Also keeping baking soda in a feed bowl in the goat pen as a treat. The baking soda aids in preventing bloat and treating it organically if a goat develops it. Moreover, many goat keepers add baking soda on the daily grain rations to prevent bloat.

5. Fiber Production by Goats

Most goats are kept on farms for their milk, meat, and brush-clearing abilities. Nevertheless, there is another type of goat husbandry that can be equally lucrative and satisfying: fibre goats. While sheep remain the predominant fibre animal in the United States, fibre goat farming is gaining popularity and providing many small herd owners with a major source of supplemental income. Depending on where you live and farm, it will be more challenging to obtain a fibre goat to establish a herd than it will be to find a high-quality breed of meat, dairy, or miniature goat.

Best Fiber Goat Varieties

- Cashmere is a goat variety of standard size.

- Cashmere is a goat breed of standard size, although it is not a legitimate breed.

- Pygora - Miniature fibre goat breed produced by breeding an Angora doe or nanny goat with a Pygmy Billy goat.

- Nigora - A breed of miniature fibre goat established by breeding an Angora nanny or doe with a Nigerian Dwarf Billy goat.

If your goat farming enterprise will contain fibre goats, knowing how to shear them on your own can not only make your homestead more self-sufficient but also save you money.

NIGERIAN MIDGET GOAT FOOD REQUIREMENTS

1. Water

Provide Hygienic water must constantly be accessible to goats. Keep in mind that your Nigerian Dwarf goats will require more water than usual during warm weather and during lactation.

2. Feed and forage

The Nigerian Dwarf enjoys eating shrubs, weeds, herbs, and leaves.

Giving them unlimited access to pasture gives them with the required activity to preserve their wellness and prevent health issues. Procure the highest-quality hay for the nutritious goats and best-tasting milk. Due to its high mineral content, alfalfa hay is essential for the milk production and growth of goat kids. Many individuals supplement other grasses with alfalfa granules because alfalfa hay is prohibitively expensive. Although it is not necessary, grain is an excellent source of supplemental nutrition for goats that produce milk.

3. Supplements

Depending on the flora in your field, the structure of the soil qualities, and the nutritional value of your hay, your goats may require mineral supplements. If you provide animals with a substantial caloric intake, they may only require trace amounts of vital minerals. Free-fed goats will ingest only the minimum amount of vitamin supplements required. To add diversity to the diet of your Nigerian Dwarf goats, you may also feed them fruit and vegetable scraps.

HOW TO CUT GOAT HAIR?

Like sheep, goats are sheared twice annually. Spring and early autumn are the typical dates for shearing. It is recommended not to shear goats too early in the spring or too late in the fall since they will be too cold without their hair, even if you place them in goat coats to shield them from the elements. It is probably okay to vary from the suggested shearing times if you live in a climate where the temperature remains relatively constant throughout the year. This is done to prevent the goats from becoming too large and their mohair and cashmere from becoming so long that it becomes matted or knotted.

INSTRUCTIONS

1. A couple of weeks before to shearing the herd, the goats should be washed and treated for parasites.

2. Shearing requires that goats are always clean and dry. A damp goat's mohair or cashmere will become

entangled in the shears, causing the animal pain and the shearer to spend a great deal more time and effort attempting to accomplish the process. Even mild rain can make the goat hair excessively moist for good shearing. For optimal and painless results, do not shear a goat that has been wet in any way within the previous twenty-four hours.

3. The youngest members of the herd should be shorn first. Mohair and cashmere produced by babies and young goats is softer and more valuable than that of mature goats. Before continuing with the older members of the herd, identify and set

aside the softest goat fleece from the baby goats.

4. Prior to shearing, remove as much debris and dirt from the goat fleece as possible using a hairdryer or air compressor hose with the heat setting set to the lowest setting. Never direct the air directly downwards into the goat; instead, tilt it to the side to avoid driving small particles deeper into the mohair or cashmere. Blowing air downwards or retaining pressured air too close to the goat will cause the fine hair to tangle, creating issues and the possibility for harm during shearing.

5. Begin the shearing of a goat by clipping a single strip down the

backbone in the direction of the withers.

6. Also, shear the opposite side of the goat along its spine. Nevertheless, this time, keep the blades of the shearing tool parallel to avoid them from slicing through the goat's skin as you work along the animal's side.

7. To avoid nicking the thin flesh that surrounds and runs along the shoulder bones, shave the shoulder region in an up-and-down motion rather than from side to side.

8. When shearing the rear legs of the fibre goat, particular care must be taken to avoid severing the leg tendons.

9. Go slowly and carefully when clipping the testicles, penis, udders, and teats when shearing the underbelly of the goat. Before beginning to shear near these sensitive areas, ensure you have adequate lighting and have positioned the goat high enough on a shearing – milking platform to see the entire shearing area.

10. Whether any of the fibre goats possess wattles, the animal's head and chest must be sheared with greater care. Always do a thorough examination of each goat's complete body to discover any abrasions created during shearing. Even tiny cuts should be washed and treated

with a triple antiseptic solution or sprayed with Blu-Kote to avoid infection. In a short time, an infected wound subjected to animal faeces and other highly toxic substances may develop a fatal infection. When their herds are tied, many fibre goat farmers and dairy goat farmers conduct full health inspections, deworm, and administer vaccinations.

CHAPTER THREE

NIGERIAN MIDGET GOAT HOUSING NEEDS

Most goats need refuge at night as
well as during inclement weather.
Position one's habitation far away
from your fence to prevent goats from
jumping over it, and avoid locating it
on lower slopes that would
accumulate rain. Many persons
believe that a regular dog house is
suitable for a doe or buck of the

Nigerian Dwarf breed. A dry earth floor is preferred to a timber one since mahogany can become soft if covered with soil or animal manure, which might injure a goat or create foot difficulties.

1. Pasture

Rotate your goats' grazing pastures to prevent overuse and the proliferation of less acceptable feed for optimal outcomes. If it is not an option, try multispecies grazing, since the plants chosen by one type of livestock are not liked by another.

2. Accommodation

Most goats only require a modest shelter to protect them from precipitation and snow. An enclosed shed or similar structure will suffice. Children are an exception, whether they are raised by hand or allowed to suckle from their mothers. Does and young should have shelters with four walls and no drafts, unless in temperate regions. If your winters are very severe, you should give your goats with a barn or shed with four sides.

3. Fencing

Goats are Houdini-like by nature. You must erect fencing to keep your caprines secure in your pastures and out of your neighbors' yards and gardens. Electric fencing and woven wire topped with boards keep predators out and goats in, but they are pricey. This type of fencing is required if you maintain horses and goats in the same pasture. Set up portable electric fencing with powerful energizers if you move your goats to other forage sites. Weak electric shocks allow goats to breach electric fencing.

4. Predator Control

Both domestic and wild predators provide a threat to your goats. The former consists of canines, possibly including your own. The latter include, depending on the region, coyotes, bobcats, and other large carnivores. Although fencing is your first line of defense, you may like to add a guard animal for added security.

If raised with livestock from a young age, certain dog breeds, such as the Great Pyrenees and the Komondor, have the innate ability to serve as guard dogs. Adding a donkey to your herd can defend it from wild donkeys, but it may attack your nice, non-predatory dog. Llamas can also provide some protection from predators.

SPAWNING NIGERIAN MIDGET GOATS

Before breeding Nigerian Dwarf breed chickens, it is recommended that you wait until they are 8 to 12 months of age. Goats are important and will go into heat if introduced to a male, so till you're prepared to mate with them, it is essential that you keep immature does away from bucks. Remember that bucks can breed as early as two months of age, and keep them apart from does to avoid unwanted births. Females are capable of producing three to four (and sometimes even five) young per pregnancy. As a doe enters estrus, she will typically display the following behaviors:

- Tail flagging

- Mucosal or discharge
  symptoms
- Swollen rear end
- Increased or unusual yelling or
  bleating

Typically, if she is exposed to a buck, she will become more interested in him and actively seek him out. Nigerian Dwarf goats produce enough milk for approximately 300 days every generation and reproduce throughout the year, as opposed to solely during certain seasons. This is beneficial to their polyestrous character. If you want a steady supply of tasty, elevated goat milk, you simply need a few does and to space out their breeding. It is recommended, if you plan to breed Nigerian Dwarf goats, that you establish a similarity in their milk supply because of the substantial potential for having five kids per kidding; a doe might very well bear children to even more children than they can help and support, and possessing someone else producing milk doe on side enables for cultivating or feeding the baby. Keeping Nigerian Dwarf goats presents the same challenges as any other type of goat husbandry. While isolating the goat from the others so that they don't breed too early or too often. Even relatively little Nigerian Dwarf bucks can be rather persistent while trying to mate with a susceptible doe, thus their cage must be exceedingly robust. Even does who must be removed from the flock have social requirements and must be maintained with similar animals or a buck. Yet, unlike most other species, Nigerian Dwarf bucks are much more placid and manageable, making them easier to restrain or retain. If you choose to retain a buck, he should not split a barrier with does. Being creative, it is relatively unusual for goats to reproduce through fences. Create obstacles of at least 15 feet between the compartment for the buck and the fully enclosed for the does. This border fence is going to prevent unwanted procreation through the common fence, but also prevent him from attempting to attack the wall and trying to put additional strain on it. Alternately, users can discover a partner with a buck and established regular intervals "deadlines" for ones is doing during the period to allow them to come into season and breed. This is a common approach for ensuring constant milk output without eliminating the cost and trouble of having a buck.

GUIDELINES FOR HANDLING NIGERIAN MIDGET GOATS

Regardless of their tiny size, Nigerian Dwarf goats require a vast amount of space to live and roam. This species is resilient and can quickly escape from their confined zones if they are weak. Ensure you select a robust and tall fence. When you want to start a farm, you must start with a minimal level of two animals to give them a companion.

CHAPTER FOUR

HOW TO CARE FOR A PREGNANT DWAFT GOATS

The duration of a doe's pregnancy is 150 days, or five months. The pregnant goat can milk pending two months preceding to her delivery date. In spite of the fact that they begin to dry out naturally at this time, it is essential to stimulate it. To dry out a goat, one just simply milk it less. You can reduce milk consumption from every other day to every few days, but by then you won't want to drink it. At this point, the milk will taste salty due to the excessive mineral buildup.

Ensure that, during the last two months, they have been dewormed by herbal means and that you have supplemented their food with kitchen scraps. At this time, fruits and vegetables can be enjoyable treats and provide a nutritional boost. You can also provide a small amount of organic grain as a reward, but don't give too much.   Grain is difficult to digest and can be acidic for a goat's body. Some people say that animals with rumen stomachs shouldn't consume grain at all, but I think a little bit every now and again is good. In order to facilitate digestion, I will additionally soak the grain or sprout it beforehand.

Running your fingers along a doe's spine all the way to her tail is an indication that she is near to giving birth. See if you can squeeze the ligament right before to her tail as you approach the tail. You may notice a significant loosening of that ligament if you do this approximately two to three weeks before delivery. If you feel that the item is entirely gone, you can expect delivery within a few days.

WHAT TO DO BEFORE AND DURING GIVING BIRTH

1. A fresh pail of clean, slightly warmed water for the mother to sip. Even when they are thirsty, my does typically refuse to drink cold water since it may upset their stomachs.

2. A second bucket of clean water to rinse hands, soiled instruments, etc. This does not qualify as a clean condition. Soap will be required. This is done to eliminate extra grime.

3. Use scissors and dental floss or another fine string to knot off the umbilical cord.

4. Iodine for use in coloring the umbilical stump

5. To reduce the risk of infection, gloves are worn.

6. Towels made of terry fabric or microfiber for drying the baby. In addition to cleaning your hands and instruments, you will also need to clean up the mess.

7. lubricants comparable to KY jelly. Please refrain from using Vaseline and other petroleum jellies. There is evidence that they exacerbate infections, at least among humans. If all goes well, you won't require this. Yet, it must be on hand in case circumstances change. The bulk of the time, there is no reason to place your hands within the mother. More on this later.

8. Colostrum mixture in a bottle with a nipple for feeding, in the event that

the infant is unable to suckle. If a bottle or dummy is unavailable, you can alternatively feed the child with a syringe.

9. grains or other high-energy foods for mum. Combine with warm water and molasses. Excellent energy boost while rehydrating the mother.

Things that are not necessary although desirable

1. A step stool which is comfortable to sit rather than sitting on the floor.

2. Thermometer which will help you take a baby goat's temperature.

3. Scales: It's will help in making predictions about the child, but they are not required.

4. A bulb used to remove fluids from the baby's throat and/or nose. Have never required one. The issue has been resolved by drying off the infant and allowing the mother to do her job.

5. Electrolyte drench

6. Selenomethionine E gel

7. Warming lamps, hair dryers, and other such products. Again, these items are not necessary; a towel for drying and the mother's warmth will suffice.

THINGS TO AVOID AT KIDDING TIME

There is almost never a reason to place your fingers inside a pregnant doe to determine if labor is progressing as it would in a human.

Because if you're wrong and she's not in labor, the baby may not be in position yet because it's too early. Unless you are a goat veterinarian with hundreds of goat births under your belt, it is unlikely that you could tell the difference by touch. Infection-causing germs can be pushed into the birth canal. There are already sufficient germs in the environment; there is no need to intentionally inject them into the laboring doe. You can cause harm to the mother if you are too rough, for instance by snagging and tearing the vaginal wall with your fingernails.

- Become impatient and exert effort to hasten the process.

When you pull, the doe will simultaneously push. The veterinarian informed that an owner "assisted" his doe during what appeared to be a regular birth. The man ripped the uterus apart as he extracted the infant, causing peritonitis and death.

- Avoid panic.